Contents

Foreword

Manchester was a very interesting place to watch buses.

Actually, Greater Manchester was an even better place to watch buses. From the mills of Wigan to the foothills of the Pennines, this 30-mile-wide patch of industrial centre, suburban garden and even rural farms encompassed everything that was fascinating about road passenger transport. It had lowbridge buses, old-fashioned buses, up-to-date buses; modern liveries and traditional liveries, of almost every hue; and it had Leylands by the hundred, AECs, Guys, Daimlers, even a sprinkling of Atkinsons and Albions.

This slim volume doesn't set out to be a definitive history in any shape or form, nor does it pretend to be especially knowledgeable on every single aspect of the vehicles, routes or operations. Instead, it is a celebration of the fascinating buses of this region, created from the viewpoint of someone standing by the kerbside or a passenger. All the photographs in this book are drawn from the archives of the Museum of Transport, Greater Manchester, or the volunteers of the Greater Manchester Transport Society, of whom I am one. The society and its museum of transport in a former bus garage in Boyle Street, Cheetham, keep the memories alive through their extensive collections of photographs, documents, bus stops, ticket machines and, not least, the buses that once plied the streets of Greater Manchester.

So clutch your Saver Seven or ClipperCard in your hand, put your arm out clearly for the driver, and enjoy the ride.

The Beginning – Before SELNEC

To understand why the Greater Manchester region had such a rich tapestry of buses, you have to go back many years – to the early nineteenth century. Londoners make much of Mr Shillibeer and his omnibus of 1829, but any Mancunian with a knowledge of buses will tell you that John Greenwood, a toll keeper of Pendleton, beat him by five years with a service from Pendleton toll bar to town in 1824. And, whereas Shillibeer was a financial failure and eventually fled to Paris to escape his creditors, John Greenwood's family business prospered throughout the Victorian age. They had horse buses and horse trams in many parts of Manchester, as cotton made the region great, prosperous, and populous, with more people drawn to the area.

The Tramways Act of 1870 didn't allow the new town boroughs to operate horse tramway systems, but it did make it possible for many of them to build a system and lease it to a private company, who would run the trams. The Manchester Carriage & Tramway Company, the oak grown from John Greenwood's 1824 acorn, swept up many of the concessions, especially in the city of Manchester and in Salford, Stretford and Stockport; while other concerns ran (with varying degrees of success) in places further afield. Steam trams clanked through the streets of Wigan, Bury, Rochdale and Oldham. A change in the law and the impending expiry of the operating leases gave the municipal boroughs an opportunity around the turn of the twentieth century, and the systems were compulsorily purchased (with a fair bit of haggling) and converted to the new electric traction, creating a nice solid springboard for the new municipal power station.

Over time, each significant town and city of Greater Manchester created its own traditions, style, fares, uniforms, staff terms and conditions – and, to get out of sequence for a moment, these varying traditions were quite some knot to unpick when SELNEC finally brought them all together. After the Great War, buses came, which were much more flexible than the trams; so did private bus companies, some large and responsible like North Western and Lancashire United, and some very small, out to make a bob or two and not above flouting local laws to pick up an extra passenger.

Using a new Road Transport Act, the established operators joined up to create Express Buses, fighting the pirate operators at their own game; joint routes were everywhere and, in fact, some local operators probably had more joint routes than non-joint ones. It was colourful, interesting, full of quirks and generally efficient – but eventually it had to change.

Barbara Castle was appointed as Minister of Transport in 1964. She was worried about the big conurbations – the big cities, whose traffic congestion was already a brake on development and growth. The result was the Transport Act 1968. Among other things it set up new Passenger Transport Authorities to merge the municipal transport undertakings of the biggest cities in Birmingham, Liverpool, Manchester and Tyneside, with actual operation in the hands of Passenger Transport Executives – and Manchester's would be called SELNEC (South East Lancashire, North East Cheshire). SELNEC would take over the local undertakings of Manchester, Salford, Leigh, Bolton, Bury, Ramsbottom, Rochdale, Oldham, Ashton, the SHMD joint board, and Stockport; and it would do so on 1 November 1969.

The first and most visible choice for SELNEC was the colour scheme. The new operator would inherit 2,500 buses: red from Manchester, Stockport and Oldham; green from Salford, SHMD and Bury; blue from Ashton, Leigh and Rochdale; and crimson from Bolton and Ramsbottom. So for which colour would SELNEC plump? The answer, after deliberation and some painted models on a window ledge in the new headquarters in Manchester's Peter House, was … 'sunglow orange'.

Orange came to define Manchester's buses in the same way that red ones defined London. It was cheerful; it was a deliberate break with the past; and it was a swine to keep smart. It was also best-suited to modern rear-engined types of bus and its application on some older types could look odd, despite a lot of care being made to give paint shops instructions. Meanwhile, the whole Passenger Transport Executive was split into three divisions, each with their own version (and colour) of the SELNEC logo.

The Northern company, based in Bolton, had a magenta 'NORTHERN' logo and covered the former operations of Bolton, Leigh, Bury, Rochdale, and little Ramsbottom. The Central company, with blue CENTRAL logo, covered the operations of Manchester and Salford; and the SOUTHERN green logo was seen on the buses inherited from Stockport, Ashton, SHMD and Oldham.

The author's favourite buses – Bury's Fleetlines with Alexander bodies, delivered at the same time as him in 1964. If you think the outside is very green, you should have seen the interior – green seats, green paint including pale green ceiling, while even some of the chrome handrails were tinted green. But they were lovely to ride on.

Bolton Corporation was very progressive in the sixties with a new general manager, new livery, and new buses. 175 was a front-engined PD3, but it had a full front, so it didn't look like an old-fashioned half cab – but the drooping window installed on the nearside to give the driver a better view of the kerb lent this batch a rather lopsided, unhappy look.

Ashton's fleet was quite small, and was mainly operated in a tight network in and around the town except when on trips to Manchester, Glossop and Stockport, as seen here. It was regarded as a well-run little outfit that didn't spend money unnecessarily. It seems that soap was one of the commodities left off the shopping list but, in fairness, it's a frosty day in late 1969 and the salt spreaders have been out.

Salford City Transport had a reputation of being one of the smartest municipal bus operators around. But in 1969, as amalgamation into SELNEC loomed, adverts were carried on the outside of Salford buses for the first time and standards began to slip a little. So, while 219 is shiny upstairs in Leigh bus station, the lower panels could do with a wash and the 'Naked Ape' posters (for a book of the time) don't do anything for 219's dignity.

At first sight, this could be any time in the 1960s for SHMD's Stalybridge bus station. But Daimler 66 carries 'SELNEC PTE SOUTHERN DIVISION' legal lettering, with the address shown as Daw Bank, Stockport – the home of Stockport Corporation. 66 was already very long in the tooth in 1969 when this photograph was taken and it never saw SELNEC orange paint.

You tend to think of SELNEC and Greater Manchester in terms of cities and market towns, but some pretty remote corners were served too – perhaps none more than lonely Affetside near Bolton, where route 53 has reversed into a little piece of waste ground to rest. Ex-Bolton 12 still hasn't received its SELNEC number of 6012.

The Stalybridge, Hyde, Mossley & Dukinfield Joint Board handed over to SELNEC the longest title for a municipal bus operator, and a mixed bag of buses. 109 was an Atkinson that would clearly never run again; in any case, by this time a single-decker with centre entrance – which would therefore need a conductor – was hopelessly uneconomic. We'll come back to the red bus on the right in a couple of pages.

Shortly before SELNEC came along, Bury Corporation decided to have Daimler Fleetline single-deckers so that the same spares could be used for the town's Fleetline double deckers. Then their next buses were Atlanteans anyway. The second batch, including 95, carried the new livery with a paler cream, and more of it. In truth, it looked a bit insipid.

Tiny Ramsbottom bequeathed eleven buses to SELNEC, plus a little depot in Stubbins Lane. But the new Bury District immediately mixed things up a bit, sending a mix of buses to Rammy and bringing some of the fleet down the valley to Bury. 6401 is at Bury's north garage and looks like it's in need of some work – perhaps the exertion of its previous school run was too much.

Leigh Corporation never ran trams, but they ran buses in a nice blue livery and their number 1 must have looked old-fashioned even in 1960, with its cream swoops and shaded full fleet name. By 1970 it was antediluvian, but it soldiered on as 6001 for a while. The buses in the background illustrate the problem in operating at Leigh – most of the garage was only high enough for low-height double-deckers.

Lancashire United wasn't part of the SELNEC takeover in 1969. It was fiercely independent, operating in a wide swathe of the west of the region, and its preferred double-decker for many years was the Guy Arab, like 18, which is seen outside Atherton depot after a repaint in the early SELNEC era.

This was the end of princess parkway in 1969, with no M56 to spoil the parkland feel. Manchester City Transport 4441 was busting between Wythenshawe and the city Center, its Gardner 5LW engine working hard. Every vehicle visible in this shot was British-made.

1969–1971:
SELNEC Gets off the Ground

People tend to focus on the first repainted buses when thinking about SELNEC but, in practice, that was the least of the new Executive's problems. Perhaps the busiest man in Peter House was the director of personnel, who had to mould all the employees from eleven operators and create a single entity. That meant eleven sets of rules, eleven agreements with each trade union, eleven different ways of doing everything. Nevertheless, it all came together, in retrospect, quite quickly; although it was a diverse and huge new concern, SELNEC had something that none of the other PTEs had: the sense of a genuinely new start.

It's fair to say that not every experiment worked. Fareboxes, with a transparent box in which to put the money and no tickets, could be described as a driver bonus scheme. Off-peak 'saver' fares were tried to encourage better utilisation of the fleet by taking shoppers away from crowded peak-time buses, but the idea never really caught on. And battery-electric buses were tried, but proved to be an idea that was too far ahead of its time.

As far as the buses were concerned, the first challenge was simply to get everything standardised, and to weed out the more eccentric purchases. It's well known that SELNEC inherited nine chassis types in 1969. And, on 1 November 1969, there were over 180 buses from seven operators that dated from 1951 or before – these were worn out, obsolete and uncomfortable when compared to Mancunians and the best that had been acquired. It was fantastic for the photographer, as we can see on these pages, but it wasn't really up to scratch for the commuter. Consequently, the engineering department worked on the problem in three ways.

Firstly, the most obvious old crocks were shunted off to the scrapyard as soon as possible, often with (only just) newer buses shipped from other garages to help. So we saw Stockport PDs in Stalybridge, and even a couple from Bury, to enable worn-out Daimlers to be withdrawn. Secondly, some towns, such as Stockport and Salford, had never really embraced one-man operation, so Manchester rear-engined buses soon found themselves in 'enemy' territory. The third tack was to allow the last orders of the pre-SELNEC constituents to stand and, where the ink wasn't dry on the contract, to tinker with the specification: this meant that at least the new buses turned up from the factory in orange, and with SELNEC-style destination indicators.

A couple of these legacy orders gave the new broom a chance to sweep clean. Some constituents had stopped ordering new buses once it was clear that it was going to become someone else's problem. But Ashton, Bury and Rochdale had each ordered some chassis quite late on (Atlanteans for Ashton, Fleetlines for the others) and they were a chance to try something a bit new.

The result was EX1 and its sisters, the prototypes for the new 'Standard' bus. Eventually there were hundreds – no, actually over a *thousand* of the things, all built on Atlantean or Fleetline chassis, and all bodied by Park Royal or Northern Counties. At first we were bowled over by the novelty – the big windows, the well-thought-out cab for the driver, the back-to-back seats over the rear wheel arches. Later, enthusiasts bemoaned the thought that every Standard delivered meant a PD or a Regent taking its last trip to Barnsley.

However, the Standard was not the only new bus on the road. In fact, there was a whole procession of EX- series prototypes and funnies. There were EX54 and EX55, semi-integral Mercedes with square Northern Counties bodies. There were the first Leyland Nationals including EX30, the very first one off the production line and now preserved in the Museum of Transport. EX61 and EX62 were the electrics, but they turned out to be a bit of a dead end. And there were Metro-Scanias, bought to compare with the Nationals. These ended up at Leigh, which had a need for a few single-deckers, as most of the garage roof was too low for normal-height double-deckers. The Metro-Scanias were flying machines; when leaving a stop, the whole front end would lift up as it galloped away at top revs until the direct drive kicked in at about 20 mph. The other thing that was galloping was fuel consumption, not to mention the dreaded 'tin worm' (that's rust to the layman), meaning that they didn't last that long either.

New buses weren't the only innovation. The Hale Barns Express was a prototype business commuter express, complete with hostess and morning papers; it was hardly a roaring success. More durable was the Trans Lancs Express, a limited-stop service from Bolton to Stockport via all the peripheral towns around the region. It started with ex-Manchester Bedford VALs, which were then replaced by Seddon Pennine coaches; eventually, its popularity meant it became a double-deck operation, usually employing Metropolitans with the same prodigious speed and terrifying thirst as their single-deck Metro-Scania cousins.

In late 1969, a representative group of buses was gathered at Manchester's Hyde Road works to try out the new sunglow orange and off-white new colour scheme. Even Ramsbottom sent a bus down for a lick of paint, and here to prove it is 6403, sporting a 'NORTHERN' SELNEC fleet name.

Rochdale's contribution was its 328, which for some reason was given its old Corporation fleet number rather than its new number, 6228. Manchester-style fleet numbers were used by several garages including Rochdale, Stalybridge, Oldham, Stockport and Leigh, even though they didn't show up very well on an orange background.

As Bolton buses were renumbered, Manchester-style numbers were eschewed in favour of the Corporation's own plentiful stock of 4-inch-high gold fleet numbers. 6576 was getting old – it was new in 1956 – but it received a new number at amalgamation, even though it was already withdrawn in 1970 when this photograph was taken.

The SHMD fleet wasn't on its last legs when SELNEC took over, but there was more than a sprinkling of ancient and idiosyncratic buses, and the SHMD's habit of parking buses outdoors instead of in a covered depot probably didn't help. So some ex-Stockport PDs were drafted in to help, even though they weren't really younger than the buses they helped to replace.

Not all of the SHMD fleet were crocks – there were Fleetlines and relatively new Leyland PDs, such as 4, seen in Ashton bus station. It has acquired a SELNEC SOUTHERN flash on the side on a white panel – Southern division garages did it this way, while Central and Northern preferred just to put their logo straight onto the old paint colour until it was time for a full repaint. Presumably a green 'SOUTHERN' flash wouldn't have shown up on a green bus from Stalybridge.

In the first months of 1970, repaints into SELNEC orange began to be more common. The new scheme suited some buses, mainly more modern types, but, on Manchester's Burlingham-bodied Daimlers and Leylands, it was fairly dreadful. Still, at least 4560 is helping to brighten up Didsbury on a spring day in 1970.

Bury's last bus was this little Bedford J2 with Duple Midland body, bought for services to hilltop hamlets above the town that in some cases only existed due to political lobbying. It migrated to Ramsbottom garage and had a decent service life. One wonders, however, about how smart it was to obliterate one of only two full-width windows with posters and service bulletins.

One type that looked as good in orange as it did in municipal livery was Stockport's 1968 Leopards. Stockport was famous for being conservative, buying PDs up to the end and taking delivery of the very last rear-loader, but these Leopards were ultra-modern, with dual doors and fitment for one-man operation. 5086 was sharing the Daw Bank waste ground with an older Tiger Cub and a PD when seen in 1970.

In early SELNEC days, old companions such as 6914 could still be seen on the road, albeit as a driver-trainer. Leigh had a very eccentric fleet numbering system, with all kinds of gap-filling and even sequences that ran backwards, and SELNEC took the easy option of just adding 6,900 to them rather than trying to put them in some sort of order. So we know that this 1949 Leyland with a Lydney body had been Leigh's 14.

Bury bought a huge batch (for them) of twenty-five PD3s with Weymann bodies in 1958, complete with platform doors. They were everywhere around Bury for the next fifteen years and 6361 had been Bury 211. It's dropping down into Radcliffe on service 5, which was unusual in not touching Bury at all, running between Whitefield and Ainsworth.

Salford famously bought 195 Daimler CVG6 buses in 1950–52 and then needed no more new buses for over ten years. When some more arrived, they were … more Daimler CVG6 buses. The last half-dozen were given front entrances. When 4035 received a homemade fibreglass front, produced by Manchester's Hyde Road works, the result was indescribably ugly.

Independent Lancashire United bought fifty Seddon RU buses with Plaxton bodies. They were a bit rough but they had a certain rustic charm. SELNEC wanted to try one, and so borrowed LUT 382 and allocated it to Stockport, of all places, where it is seen in Mersey Square. SELNEC ultimately only bought one Seddon RU, but it was quite a purchase, as we shall see in a few pages.

SELNEC 6344 would have been Bury Corporation 4, one of a number of Fleetlines ordered by Bury but delivered after 1969. It was built to full Bury specification, with green interior and destination blind layout, but with a coat of orange paint. In 1970, even at lonely Walmersley terminus the 'exit by the centre door' instruction was being taken seriously.

In municipal days, jointly operated service 98 took Manchester buses into the Pennines and Oldham's buses into bustling Manchester city centre. Unfortunately 5289 is pretty representative of Oldham buses at the time, with rusty water stains below the radiator cap and faded 'pommard' paint that eventually went rather pink.

In a last surprise before takeover, Salford City Transport ordered a batch of twenty Leyland Atlanteans with Manchester-style Mancunian bodies, but with twists such as a Salford blind layout and green vinyl seats. Dubbed 'Salcunians' by local enthusiasts, they never strayed from the Salford garages at Frederick Road and Weaste, but could often be seen rubbing shoulders with more mainstream examples from the ex-Manchester Queens Road garage.

Manchester's Panthers were handsome, fast, comfortable and quiet. Also they were thirsty, unreliable, had bodywork problems, overheated and tended to catch fire. SELNEC got rid of them in very smart order, even without a coat of orange paint in some cases. Some ended up in Australia, which was as near as SELNEC's fleet engineer wanted them.

Salford had many, many Leyland PD2s and a few Daimler CVG6s with this MCW 'Aurora' body style. There was something about the new livery that seemed to make them look shorter and dumpy, but at 27 feet, 6 inches they were just as long as any similar buses. Swinton Town Hall clearly liked them, however, and had put out the bunting for this one.

SELNEC seemed to have a mania for reallocating single-deckers. Bury Fleetlines were sent to Salford; Leigh Leopards went to Bolton; Manchester Tiger Cubs went to Oldham; and, as pictured here, ex-Rochdale Fleetline 6036 ended up at Bolton, which was a surprise as Bolton had very few Daimlers. Even so, the garage made a special number blind for it to accompany it on its journeys to Egerton, Belmont and Edgworth.

Ashton's Roe-bodied Leyland PD2s were handsome machines with elegant Roe bodies. SELNEC orange suited them better (or at least, less badly) than some other similar types from other fleets, and 5445 was looking very clean and smart when photographed in Ashton bus station.

SELNEC inherited an embryonic coach operation from Manchester, and expanded it as an extra source of revenue, with heavy investment in new coaches. 250 was a Leopard with Plaxton body, delivered in 1972, and was captured by SELNEC's staff photographer on test in Stockport.

Bolton had an order for a batch of fifteen Atlanteans outstanding at takeover, and they arrived in 1971 as SELNEC's biggest buses, with eighty-six seats in their East Lancs bodies. The extra capacity wasn't needed at Johnson Fold, where this photograph was taken, and, in fact, there was no real push to put them on the busiest services – they turned up anywhere on Bolton's patch.

The history of the GM Standard bus started in 1970 with batches of buses ordered by Bury, Rochdale and Ashton getting Northern Counties bodies of a new style. EX5 was one of the Ashton-ordered ones but, when new, they were tried all over the system, including Bolton as seen here. Unusually they didn't have Northern, Central or Southern fleet names, as they were moved between the divisions as part of their evaluation.

The Leigh district had a problem, which was an ageing fleet and little chance of new double-deckers, as most of the garage roof was too low to fit them. So new vehicles arrived in the shape of AEC Swifts 6040–6049 ordered by Rochdale, but which spent most of their lives in Leigh. At least Leigh was used to operating AECs, so the storeman was happy; and Leigh, being a small depot, was able to keep an eye on their foibles and so got good results out of them.

SELNEC decided to buy a swarm of Seddon IV-236 midibuses for the new Centreline service in central Manchester, local services that didn't justify a full-size bus, and a Bolton town centre circular. The Centreline service was a roaring success, but the others are best forgotten – the Bolton service seen here only lasted a few months even though 1705 here had comfy semi-coach seats.

Bolton had a clutch of 1957 Daimlers that made it into SELNEC orange. This was despite them being odd men out in the town's fleet, equipped with preselector gearboxes that could jerk passengers off their feet when used by a driver who wasn't used to them. 6599 looks smart at the head of this trio but it didn't make it to the changeover to GMT in 1974.

Leigh gave SELNEC its only AEC Renowns until North Western came along, and characterful buses they were too. The gearbox whine sounded quite vintage to passengers' ears, but mechanically they were a smart package to create a low-height chassis. Once the driver had negotiated a huge wheel arch and awkwardly placed handbrake lever, they were lovely to drive, with a comfortable angled steering wheel and easy synchromesh gearbox.

By 1973 the new Standard buses were starting to make an impact. Chassis were by Leyland and Daimler, and bodies came from Northern Counties and Park Royal – one of the latter was photographed in Bolton Moor Lane bus station when new. One problem that took SELNEC ages to get to grips with was route numbering – there were several services numbered 10 inherited from the old operators.

Bolton had gone for 'big' buses as soon as it could, mainly buying 30-footers from 195X, such as 6628, which was a Leyland PD3. It meant that at outposts, such as Dunscar here, their capacity was a bit wasted, but the town had a lot of short but very busy routes that made the policy make sense.

Salford never bought a PD3 and only got 30-footers when you couldn't get anything shorter on an Atlantean chassis. 3087 was new to Salford as their 241 (you can tell by the number plate) as late as 1966, but it wouldn't have been seen as out of place if it had been delivered ten years earlier. Victoria bus station was also an anachronism at this time – until the end of SELNEC days, the wood-and-glass bus shelter screens were salvaged from long-gone Corporation trams.

SELNEC 1972–74: Up to Speed

By 1972, SELNEC was a household name in the region. Buses were gradually becoming beneficiaries (or victims) of sunglow orange; the fleet was starting to come down in average age, and the staff were starting to feel part of something new. Then there was Miss SELNEC, very much a product of the social culture of the time, in which a female employee (or relative of an employee) was chosen, crowned and then expected to wear a short skirt and grace any SELNEC PR event. And there were plenty of those, because there was a lot going on.

One of the things 'going on' was the purchase of the local operations of the North Western bus company. In 1969, SELNEC had pretty much cleaned up a monopoly of local bus services in the area, excepting the trifling matter of Arthur Mayne & Son and their one route from Manchester Stevenson Square to Droylsden. But there were two big exceptions: Lancashire United in the west, and North Western to the east and south.

North Western had a long and illustrious history dating back to 1913; from its headquarters in Stockport, it ran services from Northwich in the west to Matlock in the east, and from Saddleworth in the north to Biddulph in the south. Most of its territory was rural, and most of its income was in Greater Manchester, with garages in Stockport, Urmston, Altrincham and Oldham. However, car ownership was biting into revenue in the rural areas especially, and North Western's owner, the National Bus Company, was feeling the pinch. So when SELNEC came along and offered cash for the company's operations in its area, NBC was glad to offload and split up the remaining non-viable rural services between Crosville and Trent.

Its buses ran as 'SELNEC Cheshire' for a while, but this had as much to do with the time needed to integrate wage scales as it did with marketing or corporate identity. After a while, this version of the SELNEC logo was dropped, as indeed were the Northern, Central and Southern logos, in favour of an orange SELNEC logo, which had hitherto been seen only on publicity and on the EX buses that were not 'owned' by one of the three operating companies.

However, by the time this happened, it was SELNEC itself that was due to disappear after less than five years. SELNEC's ultimate 'shareholder' was the collection of local authorities that made up the region, with a large number of elected representatives from the patchwork of local authorities from Manchester City Council to urban district councils. The region around Manchester was to be consolidated into ten larger metropolitan authorities, with a new Greater Manchester County Council. That meant a new and more streamlined ownership; and a change to the area for which the PTE was responsible, with Glossop leaving (although, in practice, nothing changed, with SELNEC buses running from the town's ex-North Western garage); and Wigan brought into the fold.

By the end of the SELNEC era, this was a very common sight – most buses were in orange, with a mix of new Standards and old inheritances from the pre-1969 constituents. So ex-Manchester 3700 heads up this queue in Manchester's Piccadilly bus station, followed by an ex-Ashton and then a new Standard. And they would succeed each other along Ashton Old Road on the 218 run out to Stalybridge.

The Leyland National was chosen as SELNEC's standard single decker, but the first ones – including the very first one to go down the production line – were given 'EX' fleet numbers in the experimental series. The first few were among the tiny number of Nationals to get 'K' suffix registrations; they also received smart, polished aluminium front bumpers that very quickly gave way to more practical fibreglass.

The National's rival for affection was the Metro-Scania, a Metro-Cammell integral with Scania running units. They were fast and bouncy, but thirsty, and so eventually the National won out with a total of 182 delivered compared to the Metro-Scania's thirteen.

Salford's buses were renumbered into gaps in Manchester's series. Leylands got a number in the 3000s and Daimlers went into the 4000s. Number 3000, a 1962 Atlantean seen in Victoria bus station, was new as Salford 148, and just happened to be Salford's oldest Leyland.

The 1970s were the heyday of the all-over advertising bus. There were no computer-generated wrap-around vinyls then, so they were hand-painted, quite often done entirely by the SELNEC paint-shop staff under direction from the customer. 7073 was certainly a cheery sight and it added much-needed revenue from the advertising contract.

This is a night shot of a day service, so to speak, but it's here to remind us that SELNEC built the most comprehensive all-night network in the country outside London. All night services were two-man operated, often with permanently allocated crews, at premium fares. All services terminated at Piccadilly Gardens and at synchronised times, so that, in theory, cross-town journeys were possible.

Bolton was at the forefront of making buses more attractive again and a large fleet of Atlanteans with mainly East Lancs bodies made up a slim majority of the fleet by takeover. The original Bolton livery of maroon and cream looked great on them, while the orange always sat less happily on them – the two chrome lines had been in place for the old livery and disrupted the otherwise clean lines of the SELNEC specification.

Most bus garages have a scrap line, and in 1975 Oldham was no exception. The Northern Counties-bodied PD2, pictured second in line and still in Oldham Pommard and Cream, is no surprise, being nearly twenty years old. But the Panther Cub at the front was less than eight years old and yet will not turn a wheel under its own power again. SELNEC found it more economical to sell it for scrap and replace it with a National.

The subject of this picture is a Standard with dual doors, one of just over fifty that were bought for central area garages to use on the busiest services. But the story of the photograph is the dereliction and change of the 1970s with the clearance of terraces, while a new block of flats sits on the horizon. And the passengers who would previously have waited to board the bus have now gone elsewhere.

Ashton's last trolleybus ran in 1966, replaced by a new Atlantean. And Ashton carried on buying Atlanteans until SELNEC took over, including 5457, which looks a bit Alexander-ish but in fact was bodied by the ever-flexible Northern Counties. Appropriately it's in Ashton bus station on the 127, which had been trolleybus service 217 to Haughton Green until replaced by motorbuses in 1961.

SHMD also bought Northern Counties buses, including its last ones, which were to the idiosyncratic 'Walsall' style with a narrow front door and 'bacon slicer' sliding centre door (which on two-man services was used indiscriminately for entrance and exit). 5647 was very rare in receiving SELNEC-style Helvetica fleet numbers while retaining its pre-SELNEC municipal colours.

The last buses received (as opposed to ordered) by Salford were twenty Atlanteans with dual-door bodies by Park Royal. With their sombre livery and shallow upstairs windows, you'd describe them as 'stately' rather than pretty. Only four years separates 3159 from Standard 7007 but there's no doubt as to which seems more modern and appealing.

One of SELNEC's best innovations was the revamped training school in Bennett Street yard. This was a response to the need to train more crews – staff turnover was at crisis point with shift work, wages that had fallen behind inflation, and full employment offering easier and better-paid roles elsewhere. There was an artificial hill for practising hill starts, seen here with the school's training buses parked on it specially for the photographer.

The North Western depot in Urmston was a friendly place but uneconomical to run, even if you took into account dead mileage from rehousing the fleet at Manchester's Princess Road. So it had to close, but not before it started to look very SELNEC, including the usual incongruous transfers in – in this case an ex-Manchester Atlantean and a positively ancient 1958 Burlingham-bodied ex-Manchester PD2 lurking at far left.

The acquisition of North Western brought eleven of these AEC Reliances into the fleet, including 933 pictured just round the corner from Ashton bus station. When new, their broad cream band and their speedy nature brought upon them the nickname 'flying bananas'. They had high-backed seats with three steps up to the saloon, and so were best suited to long-distance limited-stop or inter-urban routes, so it was reasonably suited to the semi-rural 354 between Ashton and Uppermill.

EX61 was numbered in the experimental series for a good reason – it was as experimental as you can get. Based on a Seddon RU chassis, it was a battery-electric with a range of about 40 miles. The plan was to operate a fleet in the Peaks with charging up between, but the technology and economics didn't stack up, and EX61 and battery-electric Seddon Midi EX62 remained unique.

In April 1974, SELNEC became Greater Manchester Passenger Transport Executive (or Greater Manchester Transport for short). Few passengers noticed, but the signs were there. One sign that wasn't on ex-Leigh 6957 was a fleet name – many repaints in the run-up to the change omitted it until the new logo was chosen, although it has acquired its new post-April 1974 legal address lettering.

The training school was a resting place for old buses put out to grass, such as ex-North Western 638, now GMPTE training school T.V. 28. It was a Tiger Cub with a manual gearbox, and one with no synchromesh at that, so pupils would have to master the art of double-declutching if they wanted the coveted 'all types' PSV driving licence.

Perhaps the strangest inheritance from Manchester Corporation was the parcels delivery service, whose biggest customers were the mail-order catalogue businesses such as GUS, based nextdoor to the Devonshire Street North head office. After Parrs Wood garage closed in 1970, SELNEC Parcels was based there, and their vans were a familiar sight in Manchester throughout the 1970s.

North Western had ordered twenty-five Bristol VRs before the company was split, and they were delivered to SELNEC at Stockport garage. They were equipped to SELNEC standards, including the destination blind equipment. This came as a via blind too many for Stockport crews who, in one of the decade's sillier industrial disputes, first blacked the new buses and then refused to be responsible for the via blinds until given more money for doing so.

Greater Manchester Transport 1974–1982: The Organisation Matures

1 April 1974 brought a new ownership system, a new fleet name, a new addition (Wigan) and a subtle change in livery. The SELNEC livery was pretty well-established by now, even if some of the 1969 inheritance had managed to get all the way through the SELNEC era without a coat of orange. Unfortunately the colour faded badly, with the orange looking less sunglow and more sunbleached after a while; and the off-white went a bit too off, becoming a dirty creamy colour.

Consequently, there was a slightly darker orange, now named Metropolitan orange, and a slightly brighter white. The SELNEC fleet name was replaced by Greater Manchester Transport, complete with a new logo or 'M-blem' on the side, with twin wiggly orange lines creating a stylised 'M'. Oh, and brown wheels (this tended to be the colour that SELNEC'S orange ones became as they built up dirt anyway).

Buses also started to acquire depot stickers next to their fleet number. These were two-letter codes, made up of the first and last letters of the depot name, so Leigh become LH and Altrincham became AM; while Queens Road became QS and the garages in Ashton and Stalybridge both became TE for Tameside, which came to its logical conclusion in 1976 when they were replaced by a single new Tameside depot.

A more noticeable change was over in Wigan, now joining GMT, where the proud municipal operator had put green lights on the fronts of their buses so that loyal ratepayers could tell 'their' buses from others at night. Perhaps more significantly for the new and bigger PTE, Wigan was the home of Northern Counties, one of the two body builders for the 'Standard' buses that were now flooding into service. Northern Counties were even contracted to paint Leyland Nationals on delivery from the factory near Workington, as the manufacturer was unwilling to paint buses in any colour except poppy or London red, leaf green or white.

As the Standards drove into the garages via the front doors, the old buses they replaced drove (or were towed) out the back. Consequently Manchester's streets started to lose some of the more outlandish buses inherited from the predecessor operators. The AEC Regents went, as did the Dennises plus the most ancient of the PDs and CVGs, while single-deck Nationals replaced Tiger Cubs, Reliances and the hated Panthers. There was still variety aplenty and it was perfectly possible to ride buses all day without having to board a Standard, but two-man bus services started to become less common, if not exactly rare yet.

In 1969 the engineering department had got to work very quickly to renumber its fleet into one reasonably logical series. However, service numbers were a completely different story, with no renumbering attempted anywhere until 1973. This led to anomalies such as seven separate services run by SELNEC with the number 1; a separate service list for every town; and hundreds of brand-new Standards being delivered with a letter 'T' on the number blind, just so they could display Bury's 21T and 23T. At last this began to change, with a rolling programme of renumbering into one big series. As with the bus fleet numbers, the Manchester ones tended to be left alone; that made sense, as many were very busy and long-established. Most renumbered services ended up with the new number having some vague relationship with the old. For example, most of Bolton's route numbers just had 500 added to them, so it was easy to work out that the number 19 to Johnson Fold was now the 519; on the other hand, neighbouring Bury had 450 added to most of theirs, and so it took a bit of lateral thinking to link the cross-town 487 service to the old 37.

GMT even persuaded independent Lancashire United Transport, who ran services to the west of Greater Manchester, to renumber almost their entire list of services to a set in the 500s and 600s. In this way, the 51 from Bolton to Warrington became 551 and the 25 from Farnworth to Radcliffe became the 675. But bigger changes were afoot, as Greater Manchester looked to consolidate its position further.

Lancashire United Transport went right back to the days of trams and, from 1931 to 1958, it operated a characterful trolleybus network. Its headquarters were at Howe Bridge, near Atherton, and, now that West Riding had sold out, LUT was the undisputed biggest independent bus company in the United Kingdom. Its red and grey livery was crowned by a magnificent 'Lancashire United' fleet name in gold script, unchanged since the 1920s, and the company knew very well how to run a tight ship and not waste money.

It was (or at least, had been) a publicly listed company. However, by the mid-1970s it was owned by Lanaten Limited, which in practice was what city suits would today call a 'special-purpose vehicle', put in place to sell the company to Greater Manchester. GMT had an option to buy Lanaten, which came into effect on 1 January 1976; on that date Lancashire United became a wholly owned subsidiary of Greater Manchester Transport. But at this stage and for some time to come, LUT was operated separately from the rest of the fleet. This was again partly because it was simply impossible (or at least, unwise) to harmonise staff salaries and conditions immediately.

So the LUT livery remained unchanged for now; the only visible difference was that the new vehicles that started to arrive were examples of the latest GMT arrivals, but in red instead – a colour in which they looked rather well. So Fleetlines with Northern Counties bodies came in red and grey (complete with that lovely fleet name), as did

Leyland Nationals, wearing London Transport red as that was the closest Leyland was willing to provide.

There was much still going on, but the pace of change started to decline a little as GMT found its feet and settled in to the comfort of local government control and bureaucracy. Then came perhaps the master stroke, far before its time; and that was Saver Seven.

Saver Seven was the first big combined bus/rail season ticket. You had a photocard and each week you bought a ticket (from a saver office at a bus station, of course) that was valid on every single service bus in Greater Manchester, including those of thorn-in-the-side A. Mayne & Sons. It was also valid on rail services in Greater Manchester, on tracks that radiated out from Manchester just like spokes on a wheel: and it was valid on the rail routes out of Manchester as far as stations such as Brooklands, Guide Bridge and Clifton. By paying more, in increments, it could be valid on every rail service across the whole of Greater Manchester too.

It didn't reverse the long-term decline in public transport that buses have suffered from for decades, but it was imaginative, and everyone, it seemed, had one. In its time, and in Greater Manchester, it was just as well-known as Oyster is in London today; although, instead of 'tapping in', the Saver Seven was simply shown to a driver, conductor or rail ticket collector, who was responsible for checking that the ticket was valid, in date and with the correct photocard.

For those who didn't travel every day, there was Clippercard, a ten-tickets-for-the-price-of-nine ticket that you kept in your wallet. It was inserted into a 'cancellator' on the bus, usually over the nearside wheel arch, that physically chomped a piece off the ticket and time-stamped it with a threatening 'chomp' sound. Children would insert their tickets slowly in the hope that the machine would bite off less than it should to hopefully enable eleven journeys. A bigger risk for GMT was that the machine would have an electrical fault and potentially catch fire, which they occasionally did.

The one place where the transition of SELNEC to GMT in 1974 was really felt was Wigan. The town's buses were a mix of quite old-fashioned Leyland PDs, some built as late as 1968, and modern dual-door Atlanteans. What they all had in common was bodywork made in the town by either Massey or Northern Counties. 64 and 93 represent two generations of the Northern Counties variety, parked on the Station Street parking ground that had been the site of Wigan Central railway station until 1964.

Wigan's oldest bus was 115, a PD2 built in 1958 and used full-time as a trainer. It lasted for several years more in this role and, in doing so, survived long enough to be sent to the Museum of Transport when it opened in 1979, where – immaculately restored to as-new condition – it resides to this day.

Like most other operators joining SELNEC or GMT, Wigan had an order for buses outstanding at takeover. Astonishingly, they were neither Leylands nor bodied locally, being ECW-bodied Bristol LH models. On arrival, GMT engineers deemed their suspensions unsatisfactory and so the buses spent months being tested and adjusted before they were allowed to be inflicted on Wiganers.

Wigan's remaining single-deck heritage was exclusively Leylands with bodywork by Massey or Northern Counties. 22 was a Panther Cub with Massey body. The body was indestructible but the chassis type was not; so, as with other examples of the type, their service life was not over-long. But at least one survived as an export long enough to be repatriated to Wigan in the new millennium as a future restoration project.

Manchester was handicapped for decades by having railway termini at the fringes of the city centre. SELNEC's radical solution was the Picc-Vic railway tunnel, upon which construction actually started before central government pulled the plug. The unsatisfactory replacement was Centreline, using these little Seddon Midis that buzzed between the termini, darting in and out of back streets with a flat fare.

By late 1974, it was getting hard to find buses in their pre-1969 takeover liveries. One late survivor in Manchester red was Mancunian 2118. You couldn't tell it was a Fleetline just by looking at it, but the sounds were totally different and all Mancunian Fleetlines had a fleet number starting with 2, whereas Atlantean Fleetlines all started with a 1. Be that as it may, this Birchfields Road-based bus was deep in Salford territory on cross-city 95 when photographed.

Having bought a few Metro-Scania single deckers, in 1974 GMT tried the double-deck version, the Metropolitan. They were as thirsty and as fast as their cousins, but found their niche on the 400 Trans-Lancs express service, where the new flat concessionary fare was having a dramatic impact on the ridership of the service – and why not, with the possibility of a 32-mile ride for 2p?

Even in 1975 it was still possible to see line-ups like this one in Oldham garage with a row of front-engined, pre-SELNEC buses. In this photograph there are three of the handsome ex-Oldham PD3s new in 1964; an older Oldham PD2; and an ex-Rochdale AEC Regent V, 6216, which is proudly wearing its 'OM' depot sticker.

Salford could also muster a small number of green buses in late 1974, including 3008, seen on the city's Chapel Street a few hundred yards from Victoria bus station. For some reason these PD2s were given their SELNEC and GMT fleet numbers just below the destination screen, instead of just below the cab as in Salford days. The WE depot sticker tells us that 3008 is housed at Weaste garage.

Also in Salford, 3488, another late survivor in pre-SELNEC livery, was captured on Great Clowes Street on a Queens Road-operated working to Salford docks. These Burlingham-bodied PD2s had looked a bit old-fashioned in 1958; by the start of 1975, with several hundred Standards now in GMT stock, they looked like dinosaurs.

Leyland wouldn't deliver Nationals in anything except white, red or leaf green: SELNEC and GMT added the relief colour on delivery, but there was an urgent shortage of buses when the 13XX Nationals arrived, meaning they were put straight into service like this. Nationals were driven to Northern Counties, who added the orange and installed Greater Manchester's fittings, such as coin trays, before being forwarded to Charles Street for inspection.

In the central area garages, in the mid-1970s, the staple diet was the Mancunian; delivered from 1968 to 1971, there were nearly 500 of them. The early ones, such as 2009, seen at Princess Road garage, were 31 feet long, but later ones were 33 feet and were real crowd-shifters, even if few drivers were willing to accept as many standing passengers as the onboard notice specified.

Out in the 'fringe' garages, it was still possible in the mid-70s to find some rarities such as ex-Leigh 6925, an AEC Renown with one of the very few rear-loader bodies fitted to this chassis. Its lack of cleanliness was typical for the time, a combination of a shortage of cleaning staff and unreliable washing equipment, for which spare parts could take days or even weeks to arrive.

Even Manchester city centre could see treasures working in from the other towns such as 5439, a pretty ex-Ashton PD. It would never have been seen here at the bottom of Cannon Street in Corporation days, but the PTE opened up new cross-town routes by linking two previous ones. These included the 218, which had once been the main Manchester–Stalybridge trolleybus service, but was linked with a former Salford service to create a through link across the city.

A few Mancunians were delivered with single doors, all Atlanteans with East Lancs bodies, and one can speculate as to whether there might have been many more if Manchester City Transport had not been replaced by SELNEC. Some ended up in Bury and Weaste, but the rest remained at Manchester's Queens Road garage, including 1141, which somehow had found its way onto Oxford Road, south of the city centre, when photographed in 1976.

North Western's latter-day choice for single-deck buses was the Bristol RE, which was a good thing as they were about the most reliable of all the rear-engined single-deck models of the time. The share that passed to SELNEC when the company was split up included 292 with a Marshall body, and 315 with an Alexander Y-type body, whose rear is visible to the right. 292 was a short Bristol RESL, while 315 was a longer Bristol RELL.

With Wigan only joining GMT in 1974, it took a few years to be rid of the town's magnificent crimson and ivory colour scheme, so this 1976 view is typical. Massey-bodied 3296 is already in GMT orange, but Northern Counties-bodied 3210 is still in crimson, demonstrating the Wigan garage's habit of applying the GMT black Helvetica fleet numbers on a white patch to make them more visible.

Even among the more modern rear-engined fleet, the mid-1970s could throw up some gems. 5643 was ex-SHMD but, if you'd painted it blue, it would pass for a Walsall 'special', for it was built to the same design. The lady passenger visible in the doorway is intending to alight in Piccadilly bus station via the narrow front entrance door, and doesn't seem too bothered that the bus is sweeping round into Parker Street with the door open.

Rochdale's rear-engined inheritance was slightly more conventional but, even here, there was an idiosyncrasy, which was that the general manager used the low chassis line of the Fleetline to provide a normal-height bus with plenty of headroom in each saloon. This gave them a tall, stretched look, and they were a rare case of looking much better in orange and white than they did in Rochdale's rather plain cream-with-a-bit-of-blue scheme.

Salford's 1962 batch of Daimlers were starting to disappear by the mid 1970s. Not only did they have a preselector gearbox but, unlike those still in use at the time in Manchester and Rochdale, they were not air-assisted but fully mechanical. Failure to depress the selector pedal fully would result in it flying back, hitting the driver's shin with great force. Given the choice of that or a Standard, it wasn't hard to see why most Salford drivers agitated for them to go.

Most bus enthusiasts think of a Mancunian when they think of a Manchester rear-engined bus but, in fact, the previous 'box' style ran to over 200 before being superseded by the new style. 3840 was one of the last ones to be delivered to this style, and shared its suburban parking spot with a Standard one evening in 1977.

Old and new mix in Lower Mosley Street in 1977: a new Datsun and decidedly not-new 3706 wait next to the Midland Hotel in a tram-free, Bridgwater Hall-free and G-Mex-free view. 3706 looks like the loser here, but it had the last laugh as the Datsun was last taxed in 1988, whereas 3706 ended up in preservation.

Stockport's buses were defined by its fleet of rear-loader PDs. Most had rear entrances and most had East Lancs bodies. 5958 fulfilled both those conditions, but departed from the norm by having a 'St Helens'-style front bonnet; most of Stockport's PDs, and all the later ones from 1964 onwards, had the exposed radiator that looked more conservative but was far, far easier for maintenance access.

Manchester's last Daimler CVG6 buses lasted into 1978, reprieved by late deliveries of new buses. Unlike their Salford contemporaries, they had air-operated preselector gearboxes (except for a blighted few with awful crash boxes that were exiled to QS) but, even so, they just seemed to come from another age. 4638's NN sticker tells us that it was housed at Northenden when photographed in Piccadilly bus station in 1977.

Manchester's oldest Fleetlines were older than the last CVG6s, and they didn't actually look much more modern than their front-engined cousins. Manchester Central station had been closed for eight years when this photograph was taken, and it was a semi-derelict car park at the time. No one guessed that it would one day be a prestigious arena, with a soaring light rail Metrolink viaduct on the exact spot where 4596 has just disgorged a group of passengers.

If anything, the surviving ex-Manchester PDs looked even more old-fashioned than the Daimlers with their chrome-plated exposed radiators. 3699 added to the impression by still carrying large gold Manchester fleet number transfers at the rear, showing that it had not had a full repaint for some time and certainly not since SELNEC days. The location is Lloyd Road in Levenshulme, right on the municipal boundary between Manchester and Stockport.

SHMD's Bristol REs were known as 'soapboxes', due to the square shape of their Northern Counties bodies. They scuttled up and down the valley to Mossley and Uppermill for many years and, most of the day, you could usually find one in the parking area at Ashton bus station, just like 5074 here.

GMT wasn't the only bus operator to be found within the county. There was Mayne's of course, but also other operators from beyond the boundary working in. These included Trent, inheritor of North Western's Derbyshire territory; Trent 263, seen in Stockport Mersey Square, was former North Western 217, a 1966 Leopard with a stylish and comfortable Alexander body with coach seats.

After 1974, GMT kept the SELNEC name alive as Selnec Travel for the coaching arm but, in 1975, it rebranded as 'Charterplan' and introduced a striking new colour scheme. This was dubbed the 'Starsky and Hutch' style, as it resembled the paint scheme on a car from a television cop show of that name. The main Charterplan unit used orange and brown as its feature colours, while the Godfrey Abbott subsidiary – acquired in 1976 – used a two-tone green variation, as you can just see on the left.

Manchester has a high proportion of shop and office workers, who all work similar hours, so the peak hours are very concentred. So, during the day, a wander around Manchester's depots would turn up older buses that only came out for rush hour extras, such as ex-Manchester 4597, one of Manchester's first Fleetlines, seen lurking at the back of Queens Road.

The big event of 1976 was the purchase of Lancashire United Transport. Leopard 209 of 1965 looks like a typical BET group purchase, but LUT was at that time Britain's biggest independent although, in truth, they'd been working more and more closely with GMT. LUT brought 363 buses to Greater Manchester Transport plus depots at Atherton, Hindley and – seen here – Swinton.

Perhaps the most impressive buses coming over from LUT were Northern Counties-bodied Fleetlines, which were contemporaries with Standards but had enclosed engine compartments without the usual 'bustle', and were longer at 33 feet, leading to the nickname 'Jumbos'. 359 was one of the first, and had a narrow grey relief band, replaced later by a striking, wide grey area between both decks.

Leigh's last railway closed in 1969, taking away the remaining need for low-height buses; but most of the depot was still inaccessible to normal-height buses. By 1976, 6937 was a late survivor of a rare breed in Greater Manchester, the lowbridge bus with sunken gangway. This PD3 was new in 1962 and, when it was withdrawn in 1977, it was GMT's last lowbridge bus. After driving training duty, it evaded a preservation attempt and ended its days in a Barnsley scrapyard.

Even Wigan's lovely livery had to go sooner or later and, by 1977, this was the scene in the town's Melverley Street garage. It still has PDs aplenty but the crimson is absent and, for the first time, the whole fleet is in the same colour – so long as you exclude Lancashire United.

It's 1978 and 4632's nine lives are almost over. This ex-Manchester Daimler was one of many buses recertified and pushed into a life extension to cover for late deliveries of new Standards. It was based at Princess Road where this photograph was taken. Withdrawal was nigh for 4632, but this was not the end, as it was bought for preservation and housed in the Museum of Transport.

The Mancunians were very impressive buses, and this is a notable view of the run-out of Princess Road garage for the evening peak – Mancunians were by the late seventies regarded as not front-line buses and many were starting to see peak-hour use only. Both of these Fleetlines seem to be on the verge of taking the same trip to Urmston; look at the symmetry of the fleet numbers – 2144 and 2244.

In contrast to the space-age Mancunians, Lancashire United's earlier Fleetlines seemed to be from a bygone age. 102 was the last member of the first batch, new in 1962, and had a very vintage-looking body from LUT's usual supplier, Northern Counties. Meanwhile Williams & Glyn's Bank overlooks the bleakness of Farnworth's little bus station.

The late deliveries and take-it-or-leave-it attitude of British Leyland prompted GMT to work with Foden and Northern Counties to produce the Foden-NC. Seven were completed before a change of management at Foden pulled the plug, of which Greater Manchester took two. The second, 1436, was parked at White City parking ground, near Trafford Bar, when photographed. They weren't the finished article and definitely had drivetrain issues but, with more development, it could have been a different story.

Ribble operated to the north of Greater Manchester and, in late SELNEC days, a
mileage swap tidied things up north of Bolton and Bury. However, the limited-stop
services into Rossendale and beyond continued unaffected, and this X23 has just set
off from Chorlton Street on a long run to Clitheroe. These services tended to use
'White Lady' Atlanteans but, on this occasion, Burnley garage has turned out ancient
lowbridge 1809.

Ramsbottom ordered the very last Leyland PD, which was actually delivered in
crimson and cream to the new SELNEC just after takeover. It was put together from
bits and pieces at the factory – for example, having Atlantean brakes – and led a
humble life at Bury garage, in whose service we see it as 6411 here at Jericho turning
circle.

The former North Western Bristol REs were handsome on the outside, even if they were a bit Spartan within. 333 fitted into the 1970s scene as seamlessly as the Post Office Telephones Commer van behind, as it arrived at Chorlton Street bus/coach station on the 232 from Middlewood via Poynton and Didsbury. Its PS sticker tells us that 333's home garage is Princess Road, so a duty driving on this service was very different to the depot's more typical inner-city runs.

Of all the Stockport PDs, by far the oddest were the ten new in 1960, bodied by Longwell Green. 5947 far outlasted the others and was used several times for enthusiast tours, complete with battered front dome. Here it was seen on a much more prosaic duty, the 189 between Manchester (Albert Square) and Stockport (St Petersgate) via Plymouth Grove.

GMT went in a significant way for Leopards with Eastern Coach Works bodies, whose design was a derivative of the factory's output mounted on Bristol RE chassis. The adaptation didn't transfer well, as the body had been built around the Bristol rear-engined chassis, and structural problems meant that many needed either much rebuilding or even complete re-bodying.

One can only assume that the management of Lancashire United were having an off-day when an order was placed for Bristol LH chassis with ugly Northern Counties dual-door buses. They were noisy, slow, and were hated by drivers both for the rattling, noisy drive and the manual gearbox, which was not great for dual-door buses meant for busy urban services.

Bury Corporation bought four late PD2s in 1967 for use on a bridge in Bolton that couldn't take bigger buses. No sooner had the buses turned up than BR strengthened the bridge; after that, they could be found anywhere, including on a fairly rare trip on the trunk 35 service to Manchester one snowy day in 1979. The location was Grand Lodge Heaton Park, site of a one-time tram terminus.

Mancunian 1097 had had a bad day when photographed in Aytoun Street, towed by wrecker ANA 706M. SELNEC had inherited its fair share of tow lorries, typically ex-military AEC Matadors and a couple of clapped-out cut down buses, so it invested in 1974 in this powerful 'wrecker'.

1977 marked the Silver Jubilee of the Queen, and several bus companies chose this simple silver and purple style for the event. GMT painted half a dozen new Standards in this style and moved them around for the year. These included 7705, the first one, seen here entering Church Street, with the new Arndale Centre in the background approaching completion.

The first Seddon Midis were withdrawn as early as 1976. 1737 did odd jobs, including being an unofficial hack for the Revenue Protection Unit or RPU, a 'flying squad' of inspectors whose task was to spot fraud. It was easily recognisable by having an orange skirt, which was omitted from the other Midis allocated to the Centreline service.

1314 took a tumble off a bridge in icy weather in Saddleworth, and was stored at Charles Street works while a decision was made on its fate. It never ran again but contributed parts to a project to take the front of one badly damaged National (168) and the rear of another (113) to make one good bus out of three wrecked ones.

The last half-dozen Leyland PD3s bought by Stockport had front entrances, their one concession to modernity, although a batch of Bristol VRs on order at the time of the SELNEC takeover was destroyed in a fire at the East Lancs factory when almost ready for delivery. 5895 was negotiating a diversion of the 233 when found outside Manchester University's 'toastrack' building in 1978.

GMT had a habit of relegating its former front-line coaches to secondary duties in this ugly orange livery with white roof. 74 had been new as a Selnec Travel coach, but was doing odd jobs for Northenden when found in the parking area at Altrincham Interchange in 1979.

Not all of North Western's operations passed to SELNEC. A fair proportion went to Crosville, including former NW 195, an Alexander-bodied Fleetline and now Crosville DDG 308. All does not bode well for an on-time departure to Macclesfield, as the rear has a seat cushion propped up against it, a traditional gesture meaning 'please pass – bus immobile'.

By the late 1970s even the rear-engined inheritance of Greater Manchester Transport was disappearing. 3860 was the last Manchester Atlantean before the arrival of the first ground-breaking Mancunian 1001, and its withdrawn status was shown by the painting over of the M-blem. Very few ex-GMT buses were used again in service after the sale, in contrast to the situation at deregulation in 1986, and many went straight to breaker Booth's of Rotherham.

Lancashire United's Guy Arabs soldiered on into the 1980s, looking more and more of an anachronism with their bacon-slicer doors, red paint and tuneful gearbox. SELNEC had looked at a plan to ask Leyland to restart Arab production as a response to poor reliability of the Atlantean and Fleetline, but it came to nought; LUT's Arabs became more and more sought-out by enthusiasts as time went on.

One double-decker attained a kind of Charterplan livery – Standard 8230, which was given all-over advertising livery, and is seen here in Stockport's bus parking area at Daw Bank. Charterplan was very successful and, at the time, was perhaps regarded as the premier coach company in the area, with the exception of Rochdale's Yelloway.

In 1978, Bury District celebrated seventy-five years since Bury Corporation's first tram by giving one of its oldest buses, 6316 of 1963, a coat of Bury green and suitable adverts. The green wasn't the right shade, but the thought was there. Any hopes that other garages might take the hint were left unfulfilled but, when 6316 (or rather Bury 116) was withdrawn at the end of the year, it went straight to the Museum of Transport.

Unimpressed by the performance of British Leyland, GMT decided to try the MCW Metrobus as a second source of new buses. This did rather better than the Metropolitan predecessor, and almost 200 buses of this type were bought between 1979 and 1983, followed by some coach versions around the time of deregulation. They became a familiar sight on the central garage's services, and 5105 was photographed at the Platt Lane terminus of the 123.

Mayne's had for some years painted its coaches in an attractive red and cream livery, but it was still a surprise when a batch of Bristol VRs arrived in this scheme in 1978. It was a lot brighter than the usual maroon and teal but, even so, it was a shame when the company decided to paint all its buses in this livery. Two batches of VRs were bought, then Mayne discovered ex-London DMS Fleetlines and used them to expand in the post-deregulation era.

The ex-Bury 'dinkies' ended up at Northenden. In early 1980, 6389 (on the right) ended up in a head-on collision with Standard 7413 on the left, and both were taken back to the depot for repair. 7413 was repaired and lasted past deregulation, but the ex-Bury buses were due for withdrawal anyway; with damage like this, it was the end of the road for 6389.

GMT still felt the effect of British Leyland's effective monopoly, and so tried a quartet of Dennis Dominators that arrived in 1979 and 1980. 1437 was the first, photographed here at Charles Street Works, and looked very similar to a Standard, except for the lack of a bustle at the rear end and the rather crude radiator mesh at the front. They were reliable buses, but no more were bought until 1985.

New Standards rolled in at a rate of roughly 100 a year, each one displacing an ex-Corporation bus. 8125 was typical, and is seen here on arrival from the Northern Counties factory at Wigan. On arrival, each one would be checked over for defects and given a set of blinds before being used for the first time. The Daimler wheel trims were shiny, but rarely lasted in service more than a few weeks before a fitter threw them in a corner; consequently, one wonders why GMT bothered paying to have them.

1446 was one of yet another little group of buses arriving in the experimental 14xx series – in this case, a trio on Volvo Alisa chassis. These were remarkable assemblies, with a front engine between driver and platform and a very odd staircase arrangement that came out at the very front of the upstairs – note the handrails inside the front upstairs. It would have been a shock if this type had become GMT's prime choice, and a further two on order were cancelled.

Warburton Brothers of Bury was a very long-established and respected coach company; it was bought in 1975. The subsidiary's variation of the Charterplan livery was two-tone blue, even though the old company's colour scheme had been black and cream. 27 was a Duple-bodied Leopard, new in 1980, and was visiting Atherton garage for some unknown reason when photographed.

Saver Seven was Greater Manchester's season ticket, sold off-bus at travel centres and British Rail stations. 7599 tried out an unsuccessful variant of the GMT livery, and so, to make the best of a bad job, it became a pseudo-overall ad bus for Saver Seven. The location here was Parrs Wood, described as 'East Didsbury' on the timetables and blinds for the 95/96 routes that brought Salford-based buses south of the city centre.

The training school based at Bennett Street in Ardwick developed a white-and-yellow colour scheme, and went to the trouble of painting many of its training buses. The trainers beetled all over the area, but were often to be seen parked next to a source of food and tea, such as the Queens Road canteen, pictured here.

In 1980, British Rail held a 'Rail 150' exposition to celebrate 150 years of the pioneering Liverpool & Manchester Railway. GMT entered into the spirit by painting Standards 8114 and 8286 into this special paint scheme featuring a detailed rendition of the *Rocket* and the city crests of Liverpool and Manchester on the offside.

Lancashire United's last red buses were Leyland Nationals, after which the company turned to a variant of orange and white. The changeover was controversial, and crews even 'blacked' repainted buses for a while, before bowing to the inevitable. Repainted 564 wears the company's variation, plus the reversed M-blem says 'Lancashire United Transport' next to it instead of the usual 'Greater Manchester Transport'.

By the early 1980s, the GMT fleet was becoming increasingly homogenised and the early non-standard types bought in early SELNEC days were starting to disappear. This included the Metro-Scanias, defeated by high running costs and galloping corrosion. The Standard next door was raised on stilts for steam cleaning; doing the same to 1345 would probably blow a hole through its rusty stress panels.

Recognising that buses get dirty, GMT introduced a new livery with a brown skirt in 1980. It was also said to be better for offside adverts on double-deckers, with no orange and white bands to break up the advert space. Not many pre-SELNEC buses got the style, but a couple of Bristol REs from North Western did, reallocated to Bury for services to Nangreaves and Summerseat.

By 1981/2, the days of the front-engined bus were coming to an end. The last ones in service were a few ex-LUT Guy Arabs, a few survivors at Wigan, and Stockport's late model PDs, such as 5890 at Victoria railway station.

Lancashire United's coach fleet also succumbed to the Charterplan stripes and wore an attractive red-and-yellow variation. Note that these were Volvos – GMT was looking to end its dependence on Leyland and the Volvo B58 was a worthy alternative to the Leopard.

Leyland was also developing new types and had come up with the Titan, an integral built at the Park Royal factory. GMT ordered many but only fifteen arrived, due to the design's complexity, cost and the terrible industrial relation problems at Park Royal, which led to closure of the factory. 4011 was allocated to Birchfields Road when seen at Victoria bus station.

Greater Manchester Transport 1982–86: Middle Age

The early 1980s recession hit the north hard, and Greater Manchester wasn't unaffected. The coal industry pretty much collapsed, leaving parts of the area to the west of the region scarred; and manufacturing, especially the engineering at which Manchester excelled, was decimated. GMT got into a bad spiral of falling passenger numbers, rising costs and rising inflation; and a helping of union resistance that resulted in several strikes drove more people away from the buses.

The route out of the spiral was radical and political. Greater Manchester Council was the controller of the Passenger Transport Executive via the Passenger Transport Authority. They decided to keep fares low via subsidy, which had of course to come from somewhere – and this was the 'rates'. South Yorkshire PTE was doing it, and London Transport had Ken Livingstone and the 'Fares Fair' policy. Greater Manchester's policy was less radical, being a fare freeze rather than a reduction, but even so it attracted the ire of Trafford Borough, who took the matter to court (just as the London Borough of Bromley did against the GLC in London). The outcome was inevitable: GMC lost, and not only did fares have to rise but they had to 'catch up' to where they would have been if the fare freeze had never happened. So the downward spiral in numbers continued.

From a bus spotter's perspective, Greater Manchester was becoming less interesting. The last buses delivered to each corporation before the takeover were starting to disappear. There were still buses that had been ordered before the takeover to pre-SELNEC designs but delivered afterwards, notably a couple of hundred Mancunians; but these too were also now starting to reach the end of the road. North Western buses were getting harder to find and, worst of all, Lancashire United was absorbed into GMT at last and its buses were (after a period when they were given orange-and-white livery, but in different and rather pleasing proportions) now being given full GMT livery.

That livery was now changing to be more in tune with the 1980s. The 'layer cake' orange and off-white was replaced by a different layer cake: there was a white roof, then a big unbroken orange band from just below the top deck windows, with a brown skirt. The livery was only intended for post-SELNEC designs, but one Oldham

Atlantean rather famously received the new scheme just a few weeks before withdrawal when someone somewhere slipped up and painted it instead, perhaps, of a considerably newer Metrobus with a similar fleet number.

More subtle changes were taking place too. The Standard bus was now a Leyland Atlantean with a Northern Counties body; production of the Fleetline had ended, and Park Royal closed in 1979. The Standard evolved in several iterations – firstly with slightly recessed window pans, and then with an improved structure known as the 'alloy' body, whose most obvious feature was thick rubber edging around the windows. Inside, the passenger experience was darker, as the original moquette was replaced by a darker 'salt and pepper' pattern, the upstairs translucent panels were omitted and some areas that had been covered by white laminate were now black, in order to deter graffiti.

Worst of all, from the enthusiast's point of view, was that new Standards were being delivered to replace … old Standards. The standard bus life for Greater Manchester had been settled as thirteen years; this was a compromise between getting the most out of an expensive asset and the rapidly rising maintenance costs of an ageing bus coping with the effects of a hard life on bumpy roads, which came with a helping of salt every winter. So, by the time the last Atlanteans were delivered in 1984, they were replacing deliveries that were new in 1971 and early 1972, plus the odd accident casualty or long-problematic bad 'un.

The Atlanteans were followed by the Olympians, a newer design that had arisen from the ashes of Leyland's Titan fiasco. They were delivered mainly as buses; however, just before deregulation, there were double-deck coaches too, with very comfortable seats and a livery that can only be described as 'brave', but worked quite well. All GM Olympians, both buses and coaches, had Northern Counties bodies of course; as did some coach Metrobuses, the first and only ones bodied by them. But, by now, deregulation loomed large on the scene.

The end was sad but, once the 1985 Transport Act had been passed, it was inevitable. There was certainly a widespread feeling that the PTEs needed reforming and that something had to be done. The early pioneering spirit of SELNEC had given way to a complacency, perhaps; the corporation, while not evil or incompetent of course, was monolithic, slow and rigid. One example was the controversial standard vehicle life of thirteen years, come what may, which resulted in buses being sold that were fine for another two or even three years. Another was the endless reorganisations, which I haven't mentioned because they had little real impact on the passenger.

There were actually two steps of deregulation as far as GMPTE was concerned. The first was that the Passenger Transport Executive was still responsible for policy, infrastructure (that's bus stations and shelters), concessionary fares, and all that; but the actual running of buses was no longer in its remit. So the bus operation was hived off to Greater Manchester Buses Limited, owned by the ten local authorities of Greater Manchester (as the Greater Manchester County Council was now abolished), but run at arm's length. Its first livery was orange, brown and white; its buses were the same. In fact it took an observant passenger to spot that anything had changed.

What the passenger DID notice in a big way was the second change, the deregulation of local bus services, which brought to Greater Manchester a torrent of new operators, new routes, new colours and a feeling of 'come and have a go if you think you're hard enough' – the idea that anyone could set up a bus company. Many did, and most were gone within a few years. The Manchester Evening News on 'D-Day', 26 October 1986, called it 'chaos' (actually, the newsstand posters said 'choas'), and it was, for many. There were too many buses on the lucrative routes such as the Wilmslow Road and Stockport Road corridors; and many further-flung settlements on the fringes of the region found their bus was gone.

The changes were big, or small. The 192 between Manchester and Hazel Grove looked remarkably like it did the week before deregulation: whereas the 95 and 96 between Whitefield and East Didsbury, a trunk service with twelve buses an hour in each direction, simply vanished overnight. The GM Buses slogan, advertised on TV as 'pick you up tomorrow as usual', was brave; however, with a fleet that shrank by 25 per cent in one day, it couldn't be true for everyone and the independents came flooding in.

There was innovation aplenty, though: GM Buses bought swarms of 'Little Gem' midibuses to reach new parts where bigger buses couldn't reach (carefully allocating them to so-called 'low-cost units', where the drivers were paid less than those for full-size buses) and there were eccentricities such as a Culcheth–Manchester express, run by a former Royal Blue Bristol RE coach and a Routemaster. It didn't last long.

In some respects, SELNEC and GMT were just a brief episode. Seventeen years is a twinkling of an eye, and the first buses bought by SELNEC hadn't been long gone when GMT became GM. But GMT left a lot behind: the M-blem symbol of GMT is still on bus stops across Greater Manchester, albeit in a new truncated form, which isn't as good as the original. The route numbering system brought in across the county is still, after thirty years of deregulation, mainly intact, with many Wigan routes starting with a 6 and most Stockport services starting with a 3. And, hidden in the undergrowth at Edenfield bus turning circle, just inches from the border with Lancashire, is a battered but still-clear sign, saying 'shut down engines at terminus', with a full Greater Manchester Transport logo above it.

Well, Greater Manchester Transport has shut down for good, but the echoes are still there.

Victoria bus station was also the haunt of visitors such as 8434, recipient of a slightly upgraded Standard body with inset downstairs windows. It was allocated to the former LUT garage at Swinton and, although it had never been a Lancashire United bus, in this photograph it had a Lancashire United via and destination blind with characteristic 'squared-off' letters.

By 1983 the Mancunians were being withdrawn; those that remained were seen chiefly on peak-hour extras or football specials, as in the case of 1123 here. It leads a line of buses in New Bailey Street, adjacent to the 'far side' of Manchester Victoria station, and awaits a trainload of visiting football supporters.

7219 was having a spot of bother at Chorlton in 1983, attended to by service van A47. Most garages had a service van and a car-based van, used for transporting spares or staff. The dual-door Standards like 7219 were among the first to be withdrawn, and this one went for scrap in 1985. A47 did a little better, being seen later with a Scout group in Tameside and last taxed in 1993.

Not all the 1974 Metropolitans got the later livery before corrosion got the better of them; but 1430 is one of those that did. It was seen on this occasion in Ashton bus station on the short, meandering 338 to Crowhill instead of the long-distance 400. None of the Metropolitans lasted as far as deregulation.

Lancashire United's variation on the orange theme was rather attractive, although not as attractive as red and grey, and 525 made a brave sight on the A6 road, with the towers of Agecroft power station just visible behind the skip lorry.

7208 had just finished its last duty of the day, a 73 to Whitefield, and was now heading back to Frederick Road garage. The driver simply turned the '7' on the middle number blind to zero and left the rest, as he was no doubt able to go home as soon as he could get 7208 back to Salford and pay in his takings.

The 33-foot Atlanteans ordered by Bolton were among the last buses with a pre-SELNEC heritage to be active. Some ended up in Bury and 6815, the last of the batch, was in Whitefield bus station on the 488, whose rural journey via Unsworth would be unlikely to tax its capacity. Just after this photograph I boarded 6815, whereupon the air handbrake disintegrated in the driver's hand, making it a casualty.

The new livery didn't look too bad on Leyland Nationals, and 101 wore its coat of paint well in Victoria bus station. After deregulation it went to local start-up Bolton Coachways, before becoming the basis of an East Lancs 'Greenway' conversion supplied to Crosville.

The Metrobuses had been delivered in a different version of the orange layer-cake scheme, but, with the coming of the new livery, they became more similar in style. 5140 was descending a deserted Shude Hill one Sunday morning by the rear exit of Arndale bus station in a view that nowadays has been much altered by the coming of Metrolink.

The final iteration of the GM Standard was the alloy body, much improved in structure. 8586 and 8620 were captured at Chorlton's little bus station in September 1983. 8620 had a non-standard ventilation grille just behind the driver's cab window. The new Olympians were on the way, and 8620 was used as a testbed for the new type's saloon heating system.

Lancashire United 424 was a one-off Leopard with Northern Counties body that had been exhibited at the 1974 Commercial Motor Show when new. It was in the autumn of its days when seen at Newton-le-Willows, Merseyside, which was complete with MPTE bus stops, but served exclusively by GMT as a legacy of the old LUT operating area.

After Olympian prototype 1451 arrived in 1980, there was a hiatus until the first production examples arrived in 1983. 3023 arrived in January the following year and was allocated to Bolton, where it's seen in Newport Street. The body was a new version of the GM Standard style with a thick pillar upstairs to keep the other windows of a standard length, and the rear was not enclosed with no engine bustle.

Lancashire United's handsome red-and-grey livery gradually became extinct during the first half of the 1980s, except for Leopard 460 and Fleetline 6917, which we'll see shortly. 460 had just crossed from Tyldesley to Astley when photographed in April 1985, and shows off the very handsome colour scheme well.

By the early 80s Charterplan's Starsky & Hutch paint scheme was looking old-fashioned, and a new scheme with more restrained horizontal stripes was introduced. 4, pictured here, was used as the Bury FC team coach when new but, shortly after it was delivered, the Warburton coaching offshoot was wound up and the coach was transferred to the main Charles Street base.

GMT never gave up experimenting; 1461 was one of a pair of Scania BR112DH buses new in 1983. They were flying machines and would give anyone an exhilarating ride on the last 26 from Arndale bus station to Leigh at 23.00 – 10 minutes early into Leigh on a 50-minute schedule was usual.

The three Dennis Falcons, 1471–3, were almost as fast as the Scanias, but had a noise all of their own that I can only liken to riding on a Lancaster bomber. The GM Standard body was bodged to fit the chassis, so there was no Olympian-style thick pillar, and some oddly sized windows upstairs. Service 39 from Salford Greengate, along with the 320 from Wigan, were GMT services that penetrated into the heart of Liverpool.

Ribble's 1139 was in 'Timesaver' livery for the 743 between Skipton and Manchester, and is seen here at Walmersley near Bury in October 1985. After deregulation, 1139 went first to Mercer's of Longridge and later ended up with Rossendale, who re-bodied it with new coachwork from East Lancs. It was last taxed up to the end of 2002.

2190 had once been at QS but was now in Bennett Street yard as a permanent trainer in August 1985. When the Mancunians went for scrap, Eastern Coachworks were looking for striking windscreens to fit cheaply to its new coach Olympians; new ECW double-deck coaches for Eastern National, which thundered into London down the A12, had windscreens that had trundled out to Wythenshawe along Princess Road.

Probably the most handsome Standards were those delivered to Lancashire United when it was a separate subsidiary. They carried the striking red-and-grey livery, complete with the LUT fleet name that had been unchanged since the 1920s. 6917, formerly LUT 501, lasted long after all others had been repainted, as a 'pet' at Atherton. It should have been preserved but it wasn't and was sold to Thamesdown Transport in Swindon at deregulation.

By now the Olympians had taken up where the Standard Atlanteans had left off; when 3107 was new in 1985, it possibly replaced a very early Standard in the 70XX series. Shortly afterwards, the old Leigh garage in Holden Road closed and its buses and routes were serviced from Atherton, bringing AN buses like this one onto old LH routes, including the 594.

The Godfrey Abbott version of the new 'stripes' coach livery sat rather well on this Leyland Tiger, 52, new in 1983 and seen a couple of years later. After the Godfrey Abbott business was wound up, 52 was painted in National Express livery for contract work. Eventually it went through the usual procession of owners and met its end in a most brutal way, through being entered for a 'coach banger' race in 2007.

The Centreline Seddon Midis had a long life for such light buses but, by the mid 1980s, they were coming to the end of the road. 1722 spent its whole life at QS and sits here withdrawn in early 1986. But it wasn't quite the end for this particular bus, as it was kept for display at the Museum of Transport, less than 100 yards from where this photograph was taken.

The replacements for the Seddons were twenty Dennis Domino midibuses, making GMT the biggest customer. After the new Metrolink bridged the gap between Piccadilly and Victoria stations, they became buses without a real role; they were used on odd jobs that a 'breadvan' could do much more cheaply, and simply faded out during the 1990s.

You knew that GMT had reached maturity when Standards were being as training buses, but here is 7216, along with Mancunian 2160 in Bennett Street yard. The dual-door Standards were generally first to go, and none saw service after deregulation. Fortunately, 7206 became the first bus preserved by the SELNEC Transport Trust and survives to this day.

This was the scene at Charles Street in February 1986 as the latest consignment from Northern Counties was checked over. 3218 is a standard Olympian, but alongside it is Dodge 1801, also bodied by NCME and one of the first of GMT's minibuses, a 1980s phenomenon. They were a cost-reduction exercise for quieter routes, but also a response to the threat of competition, which arrived at deregulation later that year.

In 1986, GMT had on order its first double-deck coaches with comfy seats. A new coach livery was contemplated, and withdrawn 7173 was chosen as a guinea pig. It had its engine bustle faired in to match the Olympian profile, and this was the result. The view here had a shade called 'coral' as the background colour, but the nearside and rear were white – this looked awful and coral was chosen for the production version.

February 1985 at Charles Street again, and 3205 has received an all-over advert for Lex Mead car dealers, featuring painted outlines of Austin Rover's Montego, Maestro, Metro and Mini models, plus a Sherpa van – all made by the same company that made the Olympian bus chassis. The writing was on the wall for Austin, Greater Manchester Transport, Leyland Bus and even Lex Mead Stockport.

Two 1985 laws killed GMT – the Transport Act that deregulated local bus services outside London from 17 October 1986, and the Local Government Act that abolished Greater Manchester Council. GMC didn't take this lying down and, in this photograph, County Hall behind Piccadilly bus station is festooned with window posters warning against what it said was a move from local control to Whitehall control. Fleetline 7295 has been loaned by Rochdale to Bury for the 135, which explains why the blind display is less than perfect.

There had been an airport bus service in Manchester since the 1930s, operated at various times by Tigers, deck-and-a-half coaches, Tiger Cubs, Bedford VALs and Leopards; and, in 1986, it was the turn of 3139, a Northenden Olympian with some lower saloon seats removed to create extra luggage space. The city terminus changed a few times too, and at the time was in these gloomy surroundings at Victoria railway station. The buildings were demolished shortly after and NN garage closed its doors on 16 October 1986.

Surprise was expressed when in 1986 and 1987 GMT (and successor GM Buses) received thirty Metrobus chassis with Northern Counties coach bodies. They were a strange mix of Metrobus sounds and Olympian body, but pleasant and melodious to ride on. 5210 was doing what it was intended for on a run up to Bolton on the 400, when seen at Stockport Mersey Square.

We close with the aftermath. Deregulation in 1986 led directly to many changes in Greater Manchester's transport: new routes, new operators and a new uncertainty after fifteen years of a single operator. These Nationals dumped behind Bolton garage were photographed a couple of years after deregulation, but they sum up the mood of the time well – GMT's massive investment, now unloved and unused. 237 in the centre had last been used at Wigan on the night before deregulation but now, after an active life of seven years, would never run again and went for scrap shortly afterwards.

Acknowledgements

As a book compiled using photographs sourced exclusively from the archives of the Greater Manchester Transport Society and its volunteer supporters, my thanks go to the society and its volunteer members. The society, which is a registered charity, operates the Museum of Transport Greater Manchester in cooperation with Transport for Greater Manchester as a unique volunteer-public venture. Many photographs were submitted by members and supporters of the society including Ian Holdsworth, Warren Vipond and Carol Edwards on behalf of the late Dave Edwards. Dennis Talbot made helpful suggestions to the text and, with Adam Stephenson, gave help in trimming down well over 1,000 images to the selection you see in this album.

All author's and photographers' royalties from this book have been donated to the Greater Manchester Transport Society. The Museum is in Boyle Street, Manchester, M8 8UW, and contains around eighty Greater Manchester area buses as well as photographs, documents and other artefacts that tell the story of public road transport in Greater Manchester. See www.gmts.co.uk for details.

This book is dedicated to my brother Graham, who got me into this hobby in the first place, and to my wife Dawn, who kindly tolerates it.